Poetic Voices

Against Domestic Violence

Compiled by Juliet Daniel

Published by

Kratos publisher

Poetic Voices Against Domestic Violence Copyright © 2022

The authors of this work have asserted their rights under Copyright, Design, and Patent Act 1988 to be identified as the authors of this work.

All contributors have given their permission for their poems to be published in this anthology. However, their poems are not deemed exclusive to this anthology.

No writer should have their right to publish their own work elsewhere removed

There should be no problem as contributors have signed an agreement and have given their permission.

UK ISBN: 9798370068195

Disclaimer

The poems in this anthology do not necessarily represent the opinions of Poetic Voices

CONTENTS

This anthology of poems is dedicated to everyone everywhere who has been affected by domestic abuse.

Statistics

The Office for National Statistics figures shows that every year, one in three victims of domestic abuse are male equating to 757,000 men (1.561m women). One in 6-7 men and one in 4 women will be a victim of domestic abuse in their lifetime.

www.ons.gov.uk

Forward

Domestic abuse has remained a taboo subject for far too long, rarely discussed or dissected as a persistent evil in social life deserving of political focus, support, and intervention. Only the most salacious or celebritised accounts tend to make it into the popular press, and consequently, the everyday ordinariness of domestic abuse and violence is mute. This collection of poems addresses the current malaise by speaking openly, courageously, and creatively about the spectre of domestic abuse in various settings (home, work, church) and from diverse perspectives (partners, wives, children). By making sure that the banality of domestic abuse is legible, the poems in this book produce two powerful counter-discourses. They expose the psychoses of abusers and underscore the audacity and power of survivors.

We must allow these accounts of pain, distress and overcoming to wash over us, engage us and motivate us. This book must be read, shared and discussed in schools, community groups and churches. Education, awareness and empathy are fundamental qualities for all committed to ending the scourge of domestic violence to nurture.

The success of this book should not be measured solely by sales or impact. Instead, I suggest its real value lies in its 'politics of disclosure.' By making the hidden, visible and giving voice to the resistance and re-existence of victims, the mere presence of these stories on paper and ink is a triumph.

Doctor Robert Beckford

Acknowledgements

I am grateful to our sovereign Father, God Almighty who forever reigns supreme, for the vision and function of Poetic Voices. Our aim is to help sound the alarm on social issues through poetry.

Domestic abuse is a fiend. It is harmful and has long-term effects, that includes physical, psychological, spiritual, and generational consequences.

Domestic abuse is a historical problem, and it is the responsibility of faith-based organisations to ring the bells on this important issue.

As such, Poetic Voices consists of a collective of poets, writers, social observers, and members of Seasoned Women Writers Group (SWWG), that have lent their literacy gifts to help ring the bells!

We are thankful for our sponsors who have enabled us to bring this anthology into fruition.

- Aisha Clarkson
- Alison Ray MA - Alison Ray Dance Company
- Anne Black
- Danzel and Kiannara Hazine
- Donna Henry
- Eva Asante
- Jacqueline Robinson @jewelpress
- Janet Edwards
- Jennifer Roenne – www.victoriagracefashion.com
- Marie McDonald
- Margaret
- Michelle Haynes
- Marion
- Sonia Thompson
- Veronica Simpson – Back in Control Consultancy
- Yvonne Bethune – https://www.bibledoor.com

Special thanks to Maureen Morgan, Eva Asante, and Jackie Haynes, for your help support, and advice. In addition, to those who have been consistent in their work against domestic Abuse - Thank you.

Founder and edited by Juliet Daniel

1

A conversation with the mirror

Who have you become?
Says the crooked smile

> Give one inch and he would take a mile

Who have you become?
Says the shaking hands

> Believing in his charms, submissive to his
> unreasonable demands

Who have you become?
Says the teary eye

> I screamed into the pillow so my children
> cannot hear my outburst cries

Who have you become?
Says the broken nose

> Let me paint you a picture of how my story
> began

It started in 1984, first captivated by his cologne and
mixture of Channel and Dior. A gentleman was his
presentation. Not even my family could disagree and
soon after, we walked down the aisle.

> We became one.

Oh, how quickly was that undone, spun…out of control.
It started off with subtle passive-aggressive behaviour,
like a judge would waiver.

Who is this stranger? Hanging onto the empty vows that
were filled with threats and lies, who could analyse,
how he craftily advertised a false identity of a family
man, but behind closed doors, no one saw his vicious
plans.

I would put on a brave face for the sake of the family,
perfect picture, 'say cheese' and back to abnormality.
How can a man who once gave me butterflies, then one
blow to the face!
And now hospitalised.

"Open your eyes," said the voice.
                    The smell of antiseptic and bleach in the air
"Open your eyes," said the voice.

                              My fist clenched the bedsheets
"Open your eyes," said the voice.
        The sounds of the heart monitor rapidly increasing
"Open your eyes," said the voice.

    Hesitantly, flickering my eyes not knowing what
            stranger I was going to behold.
            The voice smiled and said.

'' You have *become* the woman out of many that have
survived and have now *overcome*''. ©

Jade Murray: Educator, Musician and Writer

2

Beloved

Certain groups have to deal with white supremacy
But each day, a woman has to deal with misogyny
Living with pain-filled words that are derogatory
Torn apart because of maligning
Pretending all is well, is just beguiling
The issue of objectification is a reality
Where some have used scripture to affect a woman's
dignity

Be it proverbs 31: 10 – 31 or Sirach 36: 18 - 26

Be silent, or speak low
Defined by roles,
Expected to meet needs,
I guess not fully human if coming from a rib
Just an object to be admired if beauty is his thing
Produce and reproduce like a production line
Or provide a place for mere release, no is not part of the
equation
Some women are incapable of rape

When it occurs, it's assumed she did something wrong,
it's a terrible situation
The label strong is a misleading term
To be avoided as you will not get any help, use with
caution

Many women are nothing until they are married
Sanctification is through childbirth

If barren, it is a curse or infertile and broken from,
Domestic abuse a reduction in the feminine,
Left numbed by spiritual female circumcision

There are those who blame Eve and see women as
deplorable
Others suggest Paul is responsible
Some have interpreted scripture the outcome as illogical

Submit is linked to respect
Obedience does not mean abuse
Humility and self-belief are united
Victims of domestic abuse are berated
Perpetrators are venerated

Interpretation and translation of scriptures are all based
on choice
I am reminded that I have options too,
To either stay or walk away and live to taste another day.
So, let's be clear husbands, love your wives
and do not be harsh with them, please take heed
For we were made to love and to be loved
If you want to live a life of blessings
Care for your beloved, as she is the One
That is linked to your favour. ©

Juliet Daniel: Educator and Psychotherapist, Founder of Poetic
Voices, and SWWG, poet, writer and author ©

<u>3</u>

Boys Don't Cry (Just Like My Father)

Hello everyone, my name is
I am a victim of domestic violence
I am a perpetrator of domestic violence
I experienced the harm first-hand
In my home, growing up

You see, I never lived with my dad
To be honest, never really saw him much
But I knew all about him!
How useless, waste of time, no good scum he was
A total waste of air, not anyone you would want to know
or be around, not how my mother told it

My dad made my mother very angry
I know, because every time I did something wrong
She shouted at me, "just like your father"
This was my life day in, day out
Mummy cussing and swearing at me
Cussing and swearing at, "that scum bag"
Being fed on hate and violence, I didn't realise
But she loved me: I remember good days

I hated me, I hated my dad
Wasn't sure about my mother; so confused
No one to turn to, nowhere to go
Always got in trouble, never fitted in
Everyone's joke and punching bag
Even my first girlfriends found me useless
I don't know why, I was drawn to these women;

16

they loved me but abused me, just like mum
I just annoyed them sometimes, maybe too often
Fast forward, I met an angel, she was kind, loving
And always up for a laugh, always supported and encouraged
me
Could never figure out her angle; Why was she so kind? So
decent?
I'm out of my depths I thought, surely someone like me,
Someone like my dad doesn't deserve such a person?
Then one day it happened, planning for our future
Foolish argument really, blown out of proportion
I'm stressed from work and confused about my mum
Mum is seriously sick and I don't know how to handle
these conflicting emotions, can't tell angel
because she will think I'm useless, can't cry;
that's not the manly thing
I say something – really nonsensical
She gently says, "don't be silly"
But I hear "you're stupid", "you're useless", "you idiot"
Childhood memories come tumbling down
Can't control, can't maintain

I lost it! All the rage
All the pent-up emotions unleashed
I'm in jail, she ended up in hospital
Swollen eyes shut, broken jaw and nose
Couple of busted ribs, our future in tatters

The demon of violence unleashed
Transferred from mum to me; from me to angel
Where will it go again?
The pain, the hurt, the unresolved, the unforgiveness
Getting help now, funny how I had to come to this place
To deal with the trauma of my childhood DV

17

That someone else had to go through the trauma for me
to get help

Growing up, I was told boys don't cry, well now I do
And I'm free – even in prison
The prison chaplain had made me see
I had to forgive my mother – no easy feat
And all those past women, I had to forgive my dad –
for not rescuing me, (weird, eh? Never knew I held a
grudge against him, buried deep within)
Crying and talking; talking and crying
Tears heal the wounds
Talking releases, the pain
Forgiveness delivers

My angel paid the price of my unforgiveness
and emotional paralysis
I pray she will forgive me
to free herself from this prison I once lived in

My name is…
I'm a survivor of domestic violence
I'm an overcomer of domestic violence. ©

Marcia Barrett: Mindset Coach, Founder of Penworship
Publishers, writer and a member of SWWG

Breaking The Silence

Today I've decided
That I'm breaking the silence.
Because I've been battling
With Emotional violence.

Too ashamed to speak out.
That's not what we do.
For we promised to stay true.

But I've found my voice
And I cannot keep quiet.
For in this relationship
There was hardly no light.

Today you've lost your grip
Because
I'm just not having it

For shame hung
Onto me so proud
And embarrassment
Spoke to me very loud

I forgive you
Because humans fail
We're flesh and blood
We mess up
We're frail

Today I wish that
You'll be free
Get some help
For you and me

In time our self-esteem
Would have grown
In time as we are
On our own

We'll find the beauty
That sets us free
As God loves on you
And loves on me. ©

Naomi: is a poet and an encourager

<u>5</u>

Broken

You broke my rib, I said I slipped
You broke my arm, I said I tripped
Broken bones and broken heart
Trip, slap, no one's convinced that I'm accident prone
Black eye, I walked into a door.
You told me it was my fault because
I made you repeatedly hit me and
I choose to make you angry

If I would only behave and be the gentle
lady, you fell in love with
You said that we don't need anyone, just you and I,
but your family and friends kept coming by

When I make you angry, and when I make you mad
You said, a mist descends and when it clears
You say, "you've hurt yourself again?"
You've got to be more careful; I reply I know.

People will think I hurt you because you are no longer here!
I'm so sorry, my love.
This nest is empty that was once filled with our love
What happened, I wish I could turn back the hands of time
I'm broken without you.
He says he's sorry, this time its true,
I can see the bible I left behind, worn and tear-stained
I can now see he has truly changed, as my leaving allowed us
both to heal. ©

21

Christine Banton: Founder of Azi Sorrel and Chaniel Community Project; Actress; Comedian, writer and a member of SWWG

6

Cycles

Born into a family of violence.
I learnt at a young age how to stay silent.

My family was so dysfunctional, yet from the outside, this
was never the perception.

Sadness and confusion was behind those closed doors, but
to everyone else, we played this game of deception.

Grown up in a world of lies and pretence.
We had to smile and blend into a life that made no sense.

I looked forward, forward, forward with hope. Hope for
new life. Hope of a stable future.

A time will come where I will be able to delete all these
memories from my mind like a computer.

I finally escaped my situation, only to find myself right
back in something similar.

I made promises to myself, that I would never be a doormat
like my mother.

Words!...Words! Oh, those words that cut deep like a knife.
Left alone with the feelings of not wanting to live this life.

Scars! ..Scars! Oh, those scars that are invisible.

No one is able to see just how wounded I am on the inside,
No hope of anything changing at that time, feeling like my life is just inevitable.

Felt like my head was drowning while I struggled above the surface in despair.

Trapped within my own thoughts,
Not realising at the time that I had many avenues of support.

"You should be grateful!" "No one else will put up with you!"
I would pause with fear inside, wondering if this could be true?

The never-ending pattern of repeated actions.
I tried to focus on the positives, giving myself a distraction.

A slap or a punch, a shove or a kick!
Trying to convince myself that it's not all bad, as the reality is too hard to admit.

I guess this is my life, that's just how it is,
Things will never change, so best I get used to it.

Learning to not anger him, life is so much easier when you just submit.

Let him think he's right, don't answer back and keep quiet.

I didn't realise my son was learning these behaviours. He began repeating words and scenarios that were all too familiar.
I'm filled with fear of seeing history repeat itself.

Screaming out from the inside but making no sound on the outside, desperately wanting some help.

Those triggers, triggers! All those triggers that still remind me of the past.

How long will this nightmare last?
The smashing of furniture,

The aggression in his voice.
The intimidation and feeling like I had no choice.
That look on his face that I'll never forget.
Feels like a Deja-vu because I've been here before, only this time, it's my son!

This is MY son! My child that I carried tenderly inside.
I nursed and nurtured him on my breasts and felt such loving pride.

The anxiety hits me as I panic about being in the same situation.
A well brought up young man, with violence taught to him from such a young age.
I sat back on my chair and pondered on this sad revelation.

History has repeated itself. He has become a young man, but turned out like his father.
I'm conflicted with my feelings, thinking which One I would rather?

I've heard so many times, Domestic violence!
Walk away when you see the signs.

But sometimes, it's not that easy, you have to read
between the lines.

A mother's love for her child is meant to be
unconditional.
That bond and attachment to her child can also be
provisional.

I find myself left with only one option.
Loving him still dearly, but only from a distance.

When people ask me now, 'How do you feel about
what's happened?'
My answer will always be `Empowered!' I'm no longer
surviving, I'm a survivor! ©

Heather Annan: Engagement Officer and Trustee for HIT
(Hope in Tottenham) and a member of SWWG

7

Domestic Silence

I don't truly know why she caused me to do that, I mean to
react that way
I just wish they'd leave me the hell alone,
after all, it wasn't you that got beaten up when things wasn't
right at home,
had to shut up and just listen to what they say, and just deal
wid it anyway and don't you dare think of bringing
up a fight
Come that certain time in the evening, before she got home,
I'd better make sure that all was tidied, and everything was
put in place, or get a trashing

I never told anyone this, just brave up and hope it would
stop, my siblings never helped me, so I just toughened up
Being the older One, I had to make sure things were good at
home,
Ensure the place clean and tidy, nothing broken or
damaged...
Most times, fretting, hoping I didn't forget anything
This was most of my childhood, at times, things were cool...

Twenty years on, I have my own place, well we,
As in me and my girlfriend Grace, I really liked her,
She was pretty cool, and she gets me
We've been seeing each other for a little while now,
And it seems we wanted similar things,
So she thought, why don't we live together and hopefully
make a future

Well, I wasn't really sure, but I thought, alright then, let's
give it a go,
After all, she was nice and all, we were coming to
realise,
how we do things different around the home, she was
really laid back,
I was fussy, to me things had to be in their proper place,
At times she'd say to me, "just relax, stop screwing up
your face"
Sometimes I'd just walk out the room, because I'd feel
small, feeling like a goon, for a while, when these
occasions occur, I'd get upset,

At times we'd argue as to why she'd kept leaving a mess
She'd respond, it's not a contest, as to who could clean
up the best,
Or tidy the whole house and leave it spotless
This went on for some time, I thought one day, hopefully
I'd be able to put these things behind, from time to time,
we'd argued,
Other times, we'd joke about it after
Another day came, she shouted at me and said,
"you're becoming a pest"!!
At this remark, I swung and smashed the lamp standing
by the wall
In an angered state, I went over to her and said,
"watch your mouth, don't call me no pest",
She replied, "try your best, you better clean up that
mess"
Suddenly without warning, I felt a rush, a rage of fear
and anger came over me,
Grace was standing in front of me, in her hand with the
broken lamp stand

I in a mental moment, locked up inside with the dread and
fear of being beaten up,
I reacted, grabbed the lampstand from Grace, swung and...
ran out the room
It was only a moment, but it seemed like this locked-up
nightmare, had unlocked the mental-emotional pain again and
was ready to party with personalities
I felt doomed, when I recalled and realised what just
happened, I froze behind the door,
I didn't want to see, what could this be, felt I didn't want to be
there no more

Because I couldn't undo the damage done
The dread, the fear, how much more can I endure, how much
longer can I run
I kept tripping over the same thing, I felt the wires inside me
short-circuiting,
Something was broken, I kept hoping it would just go away,
as I cried inside day by day,
but it seemed no one would answer me, scared no one would
want to hear what I had to say
Do I remain silent, and pretend it's not, for if I can't fix this,
maybe get a gun, pull on the trigger several times, or just
once

I now know I need help, from suppressed trauma from
childhood to adulthood, hopefully, someone would hear me
and help me,
It was there and then, I decided, that I would no longer be
silent.
For if it's not heard, identified or addressed, it can become
worse than a pest
It can also become a tragedy,

Through long term, unresolved hurts and abuse kept in silence, can produce unintentional moments of violence.
©

Danzel Hazine: Poet and a vessel to encourage and share insight & awareness to misunderstanding, with hope to create better change.

8

Dysfunction is not an act of love

At my lowest point, I felt so strong
Although it was hard to comprehend the rollercoaster, I went on.
I was faced with fears I didn't feel I could overcome.
Stripped of my independence when I've always been the independent One.

I wanted you to be the One so bad, that I ignored all the red flags you had!
Giving you chance after chance, excusing your behaviour when I knew it was bad.
You built me up and broke me down, we were going round in circles
But this wasn't a merry-go-round.
It's like I was caught in the cycle cuz it isn't always bad.
It's like a dream and a nightmare that I wish I never had.

Forgiving you even though you're not sorry,
Forgiving myself for making decisions that don't reflect the love I claim to have for myself.
Accepting you for who you are, rather than who I wanted you to be, gave me strength.

You were so good at making me feel like I was going crazy.
I was competing with you while losing myself, it's like it was a game, but it was so unfair.
I was at my breaking point, and you didn't even care; then I realised all I needed to do was quit. ©

My name is Cherelle, I'm 28, I work as a Mental Health Housing Liaison worker. This is my personal experience from an abusive relationship I was in, displaying the dynamics of the relationship and emotions I experienced.

9
Feelings

Can you trust your feelings?
Feelings are like the seasons, they change.
Feelings are highs and lows, fast and slows.
Feelings cannot be ignored

Today I felt happy - He was happy
We had a really great day
He told me, he loved me
I smiled in my heart
This is the place I loved him from.

I did the shopping.
I cleaned the house.
I took the children to school.
I cooked dinner.
I washed up.
I put the children to bed.
I read.
I am tired.

Today we had a good day
He was in a good mood all day.
There was a point when I thought
that the day would turn because he said I never learn...
because the dinner nearly burnt..... again!!

Oh my!! did I remember- the sting on my face,
My throat and my arms.
Oh he hurts me.... to learn, he said!!
Learn the pain, to learn the pattern, to learn the cycle.
It is always the same.

Cycles, patterns, they won't change.
I tell myself I need to learn, learn to leave these cycles,
Some seasons are longer than others, sun sun, spring,
Autumn, autumn, autumn, winter, winter, winter, winter,
winter! Sun

Today is a good day, well so I thought, after I had
cooked,
I'd cleaned, I'd put the children to bed, then I read.
I returned to the room, that face I knew too well,
That something horrible was about to happen.
His fist, his breath on my face and his hands around my
neck.
I can't move, I can't, I can't, I can't.
Oh, I can, I really can... breathe again, breathe, I said,
 breathe!!!!!! thank God I'm still alive.

Lord, why have you forsaken me, why is my spirit cast
down within me, why???
I'm submitted in being submissive to this long-suffering.
Help or I might die trying to be a good wife, a Proverbs
31 women.
Lord, I am trying but his head is not the head over our
home,
and he isn't listening to you,
So what should I do when it is only me that's trying and
slowing dying

Help!!

Can you trust your feeling?
Feelings are like seasons they change.
Feelings are highs and lows, fast and slows.
Feelings cannot be ignored.

I've learned that feelings change,
The heart of man is desperately wicked,
if their head and heart are not fixed on you.

His was NOT!!!

Divine connection I said, it really was not.
I saw the red flags, but I ignored them because of my
feelings.
Never again, it has taken years for my healing because of my
feelings,
Take heed as you read, with you I plead.
To yourself be True!!

God's gifts are perfect and His words are true
and will not return to you void.
In Him I put my trust.
Domestic abuse there is No Excuse
Seek Help! ©

Veronica Simpson: BICC CEO Founder of - Back in Control
Consultancy
Women Appreciating Woman Award Winner (2020)
100 Inspirational Women Nominee (number 50) in 2019
www.backincontrolconsultancy.com

10

Freedom is Calling

Trapped in the heart of my mind
Not making sense to those around
Should I stay or go
These words ruminate throughout the day
Yet I still can't do what I need to do

My feet step forward, as they go back
How could I be in this trap
A loveless relationship, not the plan
In marriage, you took my hand
To love and to hold, those were your words
I meant it, when I said in sickness and in health

But this was too hard, I could end up dead
It's like having an enemy in my bed
I don't want to stay, I'm scared to leave
In my heart, I feel relief when I think of leaving

When I envisage freedom
It feels right, it feels like wisdom
A friend who will walk me to safety
Bravery the key,

I've stopped caring what they may say about me
Yes, I may have chosen foolishly
But I could only judge what he presented to me
Now behind closed doors, I see behind the charm
I am determined I would not come to harm
Try as you will, to get me to stay
I can tell you now, it won't be that way

Freedom is calling, peace of mind
I recognise, I'm unique, I'm one of a kind
My parting words to you...
you need help....... ©

Janet Edwards is a counsellor; Edmonton Walk and Talk group
Leader, poet, writer and a member of SWWG,

ZA Poem - Gentle Giant

People would never believe,
the abuse I receive.
I'm six foot five;
solidly set, my stature is wide.

Because of this, I'm often tested,
But I remain calm and collected.
Refusing to take the bait,
it's better for them and my sake.

Though there's a place I can't hide from attacks,
I constantly have to watch my back.
Along with my words,
as most of what I say gets twisted and blurred.

I just want a peaceful life,
one that's free from trouble and strife.
But I'm sucked in like a magnet,
constantly telling myself, I can handle it.

The love I have is all so pure;
I wish I had the antidote or the cure.
To make my situation change,
it's causing mental and physical pain.

I don't react and manage best I can,
but under the surface, I feel less of a man.
Shame doesn't allow me to tell,

full of scratches and bruises, I silently yell.

I can't get a grip on what's going on,
today I was kicked, and my clothes were torn.
Domestic violence is such a vile act;
you hear countless cases of women being attacked.

Nobody seems to talk about it happening to men,
women are violent too; I've been stabbed with a pen.
I've been living with her outbursts for many years;
the dysfunction in my house has left me in tears.

I can't believe I'm saying it;
I'm in an abusive relationship.

Saying it out loud, being true to myself,
Has given me the courage
To share it with someone else.

I confided in my brother, also a friend,
They gave me leaflets on Counselling; it's been time well
spent
I learned of other men, who were DV victims,
This gave me clarity on my isolated thinking.

Now I was open for healing to take place,
Gaining back my confidence at a healthy pace
I wasted so much time wondering how I would be judged,
Instead, I got support and plenty of love. ©

Realitie, creates and serves under the umbrella of All About US (Understanding Society). She is a Spoken Word Artist, Playwright, Workshop Facilitator, Fashion Designer for an up-and-coming brand Zephen Ashley and volunteers to source furniture and baby clothes/toys for service users of a charity and the wider community. Realitie is also a member of SWWG

He Cries – But Oh So Silently

He cries but oh so silently...
He wants to shout
Let his emotions out
But instead he always cloaks them
buries them internally
He is 'the man - the bro'
Can't let the brothers know
he's hurting
They prefer to hear about his flirting
So he lies and hides from listening ears
and prying eyes
Away from wagging tongues that travel
Unable to help him to unravel
The reasons why he does what he does
If only he knew how to express his feelings
and to manage these emotions constantly reeling
Into a chaotic motion of do's and don'ts
of confusion that drives his 'wills' and 'wonts'

He cries but oh so silently...
He wants to let go and to scream
But doesn't know what letting go means
Except through outbursts of rage
Of ugly outbursts of evil words hurled
Of violent fits of punching fists
Of a foot that stamped her face
And when her blood raced
like a running stream
Wasn't moved by what he'd seen
She rolls over with a face bruised

Once beautiful but now bares the hallmarks of physical
abuse
She looks up into his eyes with tears
With misguided compassion for 20 years
Living with the hope that one day her man would return
To the man that made her burn
with passion
That made her weep
That tears of joy and laughter would resume
That made her excited by just a look across the room
She hoped that cupid's harp would play her tune
But Cupid had an arrow instead
That would pierce her heart and shoot her dead.
When she met this man he was gentle and calm
As charming as a man would dare be
But now this other man had stolen her love
And robbed him of his chivalry
With eyes that no longer lovingly
caressed
now their look was filled with anger and distress
He was a broken man, a mixed up mess

He cries but oh so silently...
You see, it can't be loud
That's not aloud
Had to be strong, must get it right
"Pull yourself together, be a man"
Must have direction must have a plan
Must have a purpose must have dreams
Has failed so is told he is a failure
Called stupid called a clown
So in steps depression
Strangling his dignity and self worth
Dragging him deeply down

And he cries but oh so silently...
His personality seemed to have faded into grey
This imposter has become rooted intending to stay
She longed to get her true love back
Despite the continued violent attacks
Believed he would return one day
"He will come good" she'd always say
But all that came was death
Beating on her chest like an angry drum!
Pounding till it took her last breath
You see no one understood they didn't see
His internal torment it was a mystery
And one day he let his angel fly away
With no reason no warning he attacked
stabbing her repeatedly in her back

He cries but oh so silently...
He just doesn't understand
What does it mean to be a man
His father beat his mother black and blue
That's all he knew
Was never told "good boy" " well done"
Was never shown how to hug
But was shown how to hold a knife and
how to shoot a gun
Was given them as toys
That's what they gave to boys
To show them that they're strong
Girls were given dolls
Boys had swords and guns
They fight and show their might
But for some the game didn't turn out right
He cries he's going mad he's seeing red
Voices voices in his head

My God what have I done?
Stepping into reality he is filled with dread
Everything and all is now undone
He sits waiting for them to come
To take him away in chains
History again!
Nervously he waits
He knows his fate
His parents foretold that he would be "no good"
End up a looser end up doing crime

They repeatedly said he'd end up doing time
So the prophecy came true
All he did was all he saw
Was all he ever knew
They spoke it
He lived it
Who is to blame?
I need help!

He cries oh so silently...
Who can save me
Now he cries
Oh yeah now he screams
Now he shouts
Now he lets his feelings out
He cries
He screams
He shouts
Now he lets his feelings out
But she's gone and they have become
Statistics in the records of domestic fatalities
What of the children?
They'll be taken into care as they do

Will they become statistics too?
He cries but oh so silently... ©

Jessica Meade: Poet, writer, author and Founder of The Home of
Christian Poets and Creativity Inside Minds,
https://www.christianpoets.co.uk

Jessica's message: Too often we sit in the seat of judge and jury. I
apologise if this poem is painful to some - it
is meant to provoke a desire in us to gain a greater understanding of
the root causes of the behaviour of both
the perpetrators as well as the victims of domestic abuse.
Proverbs 4:7 Wisdom is the principal thing; Therefore get wisdom.
And in all your getting, get understanding.
(New King James Version, NKJV).

13

I am Woman

I am woman, created by the Master's hands
I am woman fearfully and wonderfully made in Yah's
image!
I am woman, a gift of great value

I am not defined by my hair, my nails, my age or
educational background
Do not try to box me in and think I am only what you
see
look beyond my age, my size and your perceptions of
what you want me to be
look at the One who created me; as a rare and peculiar
treasure; and packaged me with great potential!
I am indeed a treasure in earthen vessel, come look and
you will see, a treasure beyond measure!

I am woman born of love to be loved, and give love
I am woman, Elohim's masterpiece; a truly virtuous
woman; crowned with Elohim's glory

I am a precious and priceless jewel in Yahua's crown, to
know me, you have to get to the heart of me, and there
you will see my Elohim!

I am woman, I wear many hats, I am many things to
many people but first, I am a daughter of The Most
High!
I am woman, a worshipper, a warrior, and a weapon in
the hands of my Elohim!

Don't underestimate me, as I come in the volume of the book, it is written of me
I come packaged with so much power and potential to do the will of my Elohim

I am woman blessed beyond measure, loved abundantly and guarded jealously! ©

Merlene Huie: is a writer, educator, praise dancer, poet, dressmaker, cake maker and a creative. Merlene has a passion for reading, creating handmade gifts, and fashion design. Merlene is also mother, grandmother and great grandmother!

14

I made it

I can't believe I am actually here,
and you are nowhere to be seen
In my palace, I am the queen
I have such freedom I never perceived,
Free at last, out of that prison cell
Where I was held captive in my thoughts
thinking I had no power to leave and rebuild

Many nights I lay there crying,
how was I going to escape this prison
All of a sudden, the bricks started falling,
one at a time, I suddenly saw the lie
Wives submit to your husband,
be still and silent, because you belong to me
What he didn't realise was his responsibility

To treat me like a precious stone
and delicately like a flower
This is who I am, precious,
I belong to the One who made me equal to you
For I am bone of your bone,
break me and you will be broken
Love me and you will be loved

I am the Father's blessing from above
What you didn't seem to understand
was the favour available to you
Instead, you mistreated me, now I have left you
I feel free and strong in finding myself again
Every promise He gave you was also for me,

I am a beautiful and precious flower
with a spine rooted and firmly grounded
Bursting with His fragrance
that changed my life and inspiring others. ©

Penned Tapestry writers Janet, Juliet, Shirley, are members of
SWWG

15

Intergenerational Ghostly Vows

The ghosts from his nursery arrived without warning,
waving their invitation, as if carrying a VIP pass and
right of entry,
The hands he used to make me feel safe, to stroke my
face,
to carry me to bed, became weapons of mass destruction,
Punches that bruised the cocoa butter skin,
he devoured last night, and slaps that silenced the mouth
that had declared 'I love you' at the altar,
In front of family, friends, the congregation,'
for better and for worse.

His torrent of harsh and abusive words, in polarisation of
the sweetness,
he whispered to me last night, as the sun was setting
where we played and laughed together, giggling and
kissing
and planning our four children, two girls and two boys.

Fight or flight! I froze.
Caught between shame and fear.
My confetti-covered wedding dress
hanging in the wardrobe still warm.
The salty taste of fresh blood filled my mouth.

'Do you take this man to be your, to be your,
to be your lawful wedded abuser?
I thought I heard myself shout 'No'.

Who gives this woman to this man?
I flashed back to the smiling face of Daddy.
Filled with manly pride
as he walked his Princess down the aisle,
glancing knowingly and acknowledging
members of the congregation as we passed the pews.
The wedding was billed as
'the Coming Together of two Praying Families', a 'Union of
Love'.
Thousands had been spent on the event
with pastoral leaders from churches in the south-east
invited to witness this 'blessing of love'.

I grimaced, this was hurting,
The ghostly visitor was not nice.
Was unwelcome. I covered my head.

With this ring I do, I do,
with this ring, I do, Ouch!,
His ring caught the corner of my eyelid
which immediately opened,
as I had opened my soul to my husband,
and had given myself like a lamb to the slaughter.

I heard a voice screaming, 'No! No! Please Stop!'.
I recognised the voice. It wasn't mine.

It was the voice of my mother.
She was cowering by the kitchen sink.

Mummy?
Me?

Had history really repeated itself.
Had I really married a man like my father.

51

I now pronounce you man and wife. ©

Marlene-Antoinette Daley: Psychotherapist and Champion for Women's Voices
More information please refer to weblink below to know about her services
http://www.integratedthinkingtherapies.com

Special message from Marlene-Antoinette: We need to break the cycle of domestic abuse by educating our sons and our daughters that violence is not the answer. We need to speak up and out, on platforms of influence and set our people free by recognising trauma and mental health in our community.

Kupenda Na Kushikilia

To love and to hold,
that's what I was sold.
Do as I say, is what I was told.

You belong to me,
but I was never free,
that's the voice from deep inside of me.

To start again is not a guarantee,
but to love and to hold was meant for me.

I now, love me and I am set free,
against all odds and possibility. ©

Derick Dalson: Children and Family worker, with a heart for justice
for all.

My Acceptance - A New Start

I watched daily as dad used mum to play the drum,
In plain English, dad beat mum.
Dad was fierce and strong
He was my protector though he did wrong
He was always good to me despite acting violently
I was seeing Val who was kind of wimpish
I preferred a guy to be more ruggish
So I'm now with Kirk some say he's a jerk
But to me, he's really great even though he despises
most of my mates
Some say he's possessive; I see it as he's overprotective
Because he cares so much for me, why can't others see?

On the floor I lay, Kirk had a bad day
So he lashed out and slapped me straight in the mouth
And I tripped and slipped, but he didn't really mean it.
He hugged me; I felt better then he apologised for his
behaviour
I looked at him; he looked so good and ruggish like a
real man should.
Ouch! It's not that hard of a blow
After all, it's what I've seen; it's all I know
Kirk reminds me of dad though he gets mad; I need him
in my life.
Anyway, it could be worse, Kirk looks after me
He puts money in my purse, others have a lack of
tolerance, I don't
I stand by my man, I show this in my acceptance.

Week in, weeks out,
Months in, years out.

Then one day, something changed,
My outlook on life had been rearranged.
Introduced to the church and my Lord and Savior,
I was born again, and my old life was over.
As I grew in faith, I learned many truths and lessons,
This led me to many more questions.
Do I have to tolerate what I consider as my fate?
Or kick him out and change the trait
Making excuses when he's irate
Stepping to me to perpetrate
No more! His excuses were poor

I now know and see my worth don't need to curse
As I have the thirst to make myself greater than my
perpetrator
Who I excused anytime I was bruised
Now it's game over, wherever you are, you lose.
I saw myself as a victim, blamed it on my surroundings

But really, it was just an excuse to leave myself open to abuse
For I have a choice to be blinded or listen to the voice
That tells me to get out, as this is not what life's about.
Kirk couldn't believe when I found the courage to up and
leave
I can do all things through Christ, who strengthens me
Once close; now so far apart as I venture on with my new
start. ©

Realitie, creates and serves under the umbrella of All About US
(Understanding Society). She is a Spoken Word Artist, Playwright,
Workshop Facilitator, Fashion Designer for the up and coming
Zephen Ashley Brand. In addition, Realitie volunteers to source
furniture; baby clothes and toys for service users of a charity and
the wider community. Realitie is also a member of SWWG.

18

My Courage

You say that you want me to love you.
Then why do you hurt me.
You say that you want me to love you.
Then why do you abuse me
You say that you want me to love you.
Then why do you beat me
Why, why, why are you tormenting me.

What is it that you want from me?
You say that you want me to love you.
And I told you that, I do love you.

You gave me an ultimatum,
After an ultimatum and now I have no friends.
You gave me an ultimatum,

After an ultimatum and now I have no family.
You gave me an ultimatum,
After an ultimatum and now I have no personality.
What is it that you want from me
You say you want me to love you.
And I say that I do love you
But you abuse me
You scream at me
You shout at me
You are aggressive towards me
And yet you say you love me.

What is this definition of love
And why are you suddenly
slapping me.

What have I done to you,
Why do you treat me like this
What have I done so bad to deserve this
Is the truth too much to hear?

I've found my voice now
And I've found my courage,
Now, I'm done with you. ©

Pastor Lance G Jones: Author

Night Owl

Memories plagued our minds
from years gone by
sounds we heard at night
mothers voice and dishes break
while we were kept out of sight
too young to get involved
powerless to make a change
though years have past
and men we are now
those sounds still remain

The innocence of children
how delicate their mother
the only hand raised toward them
should be lifting them in wonder. ©

Kimba Bush-Ramsey BSc Industrial Tech / Drafting & Design
Performance Poet: Facilitator; Author; Recording Artist;
Songwriter; Producer
Creator of: The Flow Academy -
Educate.Enlighten.Empower.Music.Film.Fashion.
Artreprenuership
www.kingkimba.com

O Woman! O Rahab! O Ruth

She held it all together
She cowered under her shyness & fears
She called herself the person for all to come to for help
She said she will hide the spies
She said she will let them down her window
She was to carry the line of the Messiah
She knew she was a woman of purpose, but they thought of
her differently; a harlot
Her spirit said she was a warrior, a cocoon of legacy, but he
made her a woman of pain, a woman disapproved off
'Am I a warrior or victim? Am I a cocoon of life or death?
Am I a legacy of wisdom or foolishness? Am I a woman
who rescues or needs to be rescued?'
She called for help, she walked away, she took all that was
hers and let the walls of Jericho fall.

O Woman! She was Rahab

O Woman, who are you? She said to her Naomi, 'where you
go I go, where you live I live, your God will be my God and
your people my people'. She left; she wanted to leave the
pain behind

She will no longer be a Moabite; she will leave the pain
behind and start again

O Woman! Who are you? I am Ruth, my name is Ruth, I will
fulfil purpose, I will be the cocoon of legacy, and I will be
respected. I am a warrior not a victim, I choose life, not
death, your God will be my God, and your people my people

O man! Who is he? He is Boaz, my redeemer! He has replaced my dark days with hope and love; now I am the redeemed

O Woman!

You are a Rahab, You are a Ruth and you will cocoon life, hope and love, you will live and fulfil purpose Start again. Walk away, leave the pain behind, you are free

You are victorious

You are graced

For; whom the Lord sets free is free indeed ©

Jennifer Ronne: Founder of Victoria Grace Fashion & Victoria Grace Foundation; writer and a member of SWWG

21

Out of Darkness

As a little girl, I believed the word,
Sticks and stones will break my bones,
But words will never hurt me
Now the truth is impossible to hide
Another blow to the head,
Has warped time again,
How long have I been down for
While unconscious,
I was taken back to better times,
Is this why my subconscious is keeping me bound.

I used to feel the warmth in his eyes,
Now there's an emptiness inside
My esteem was shattered,
In you, I can confide,
from all the trauma I've been through,
I can no longer hide
He truly loved me,
Why did he change,
How did he change
Love is light, love is life

But darkness entered him,
When did it happen
Voices, voices, I hear your hearts cry.
I messed up when I tried to shut you up,
In trying to be a man with a shattered past
And a wounded soul.
I am sorry for what I did,
Please know you are free to go. ©

Penned Tapestry writers: Nuala, Rebekah, Christine, Heather, Andria, Eva, Marcia and Juliet are members of SWWG

Precious

I am precious and honoured in the eyes of my Elohim
fearfully and wonderfully made
loved beyond measure
I am a queen, a treasure in an earthen vessel
My price is far above rubies

My Elohim sees me as a jewel of inestimable value
a rare and peculiar treasure, so, how can you look at me and
abuse me?
Do you not know my worth and my value?
Do you not know what you see is more than your eyes can
perceive?
I am the apple of my Father's eyes.

He has put a crown of glory on my head
and made me a royal diadem in His hands
See me through the eyes of my Elohim
and, treat me with the honour
He showed me, as precious and honoured in His sight!
He has clothed me in fine linen and silk, and beautified me
with His love. ©

Merlene Huie: is a writer, educator, praise dancer, poet, dressmaker,
cake maker and a creative. Merlene has a passion for reading,
creating handmade gifts, and fashion design. Merlene is also a
mother, grandmother and great-grandmother!

Receive Your Prize

Behind the smirk lies the unspoken words
Lost in transit across the Atlantic, physical hurt
Stemming from spiritual curses, beware of the workings
The root causes the leaves of beauty to perish,
Why pretend to be full of gold when your insides wither

Like old leaves lacking water and your lands
Are desolate through constant torture
The walking dead produces no fruit
The juice is rotten from the abuse,

Ambition missing the lost inner child chokes as the
noose tightens
What's your purpose, and what's your earthly
assignment
Evil spirits conspire to lure you out of alignment
What's within will surely be revealed; it's a matter of
timing
But every burden finds its home on an arched spine
Why don't you give that load to the One they call Christ

The flickering candle of light that restores dry bones
and redeems life, despite your past enterprise
Enter through the narrow path and receive your prize
Freedom is a must, and domestic abuse is designed
to keep your spirit locked up with a heavy yoke and bolt
its nuts
Freedom is priceless I pray you purchase. ©

Boy Nash: Educator & musical artist
https:www.boynash.com

Red Flag

A punch, a kick, stepped on and bit
Verbally abused, emotionally hit
Ignored, dragged and used treated like#*?
At first, she said, "oh it's alright I fell over, I tripped."
But the whole household feels the reality of it.

The vulgar name calling the all night balling,
Bruises you get not just from falling
More and more beatings the hurt and the cuts,
Her heart was bleeding stuck fast in a rut,
Unable to leave, believed she was rubbish,
No one would want her like abandoned luggage.

She was a burden, it's her fault she's cursed,
It will soon get better but it only got worse,
Like unhealed scars behind prison bars,
She wandered will I die will it go that far.

And then there's the flip side, cos men suffer too,
Pushing hurt emotional buttons, wifey vowed not to do,
The abusive backlash from her past coming out,
As she shouts in your face and gives you a clout.

She can't help but demoralise because of her pain,
Disrespect, degrade and humiliate treat you with disdain.
Passive aggressive it's all in the mix,
She's manipulative, insecure full of nasty tricks.

Dysfunctional homes and the children that suffer,
Looking for a sedative, something to buffer,
The pain, the rain, to remain sane

Adults, please realise they feel they're to blame.

" Please, God, please, God make it stop. I'm
Sorry I'm naughty sorry I messed up "
No self-esteem, no self-worth,
Forgetting they are miracles just feeling like earth.

The terrible scenes, seen as a kid,
Those images remain of what daddy did.
" I'm just a kid, who just wants to play
I tried to help mummy but got pushed hard out the way,
Stop, daddy, please we've had enough,
Mummy's crying, stop treating her rough."

Children who suffer the torment within
Sometimes grow up to repeat the hand me down sin,
Or maybe just shut down as emotions grow cold,
With debilitating feelings as they shape up in the mould.

Domestic violence screams of silence
Unable to speak, express or talk,
But there is a voice in your wilderness who beckons you
walk,
Walk this way into His Peace,
He Heals, He Restores and Frees you from the beast.

So sound the Alarm. Give Yahushua a tag
Don't suffer in silence and wave the Red Flag. ©

Patrick Stanley – Spoken Man: Poet, Author, Voice Artist,
Singer & Songwriter

Revealed

It was a one-off......
A one-time event really.......

You sauntered into my life like an unexpected gift
No credentials
Unchecked yet trusted
Charming, romantic and that was enough
I gave you my heart

Post honeymoon,
Subtleties seeped in unnoticed
Unmasking revelations of insecurities,
Restlessness, impatience, frustration
Dominance of power displayed
Fear projected as
Raised voice meets ear

Sorry!
It won't happen again......

Overtime things progressed
Frustration turned to anger daily
Silence verbalised your inner words
Facial expressions showed unspoken thoughts
Actions followed
Hand meets face

Bruises showing, cannot escape
Cold looks from frozen eyes
Pieced like icicles
Domestic roll continues

Wash, cook, clean, obey.
Running behind in chores is a no, no
But, it happened, supper delayed
Rage torched your eyes
Fist meets stomach

Days past in a haze
I was picked up like a small child
Shielding, shivering, shaking
A shell of myself
Confused, perplexed
Feeling worthless, foolish
Not knowing what's next
Questions flooded my mind,
Questions I had no answer for
Why? Why? Why?

This treasured earthen vessel.
A precious gift bestowed to you, to cherish, nurture, to
respect

Daily lashings continued
As bruises tongued a thousand whispers
Loneliness was a comfort, fear a friend
Dread was food
Trapped, battered and marked for life
You were out, a welcomed break
You returned
Foot meets body

Years of trauma embedded
Hand marks, shoe marks, implements marks
Though silent, tattooed on God-made flesh spoke with
precision
When was prayer going to be answered?

An everyday question

A prisoner in defence mode appeared
Tool wrenched out of raise hand
Stopped before incident
Head no longer bowed
Eyes displaying deep-rooted love
Guilt manifested, a mirror
Revealing mummy hurting daddy
As I'm hurting my husband

The intensity of love
Bought me to my humanity
Disgust arrested my heart
And tortured my soul
Seeing engraved images
I was cradled in loving arms and slept.

I awoke to the sound of strong footsteps
Taken away and read my rights
Time allowed reflected memories
Shame, disgrace, dishonour
The mirror reappeared it boomerang
Neglect, rejection,
Intimidation, accusations, threats,
Control, stalking, enslavement,
Dejection, restriction, coercion
The abuses, mental, physical,
Sexual, verbal, emotional

CRACK! the mirror shattered
as it continued to reveal………
ill-treatment, heartache, pain
I now see!

Domestic violence, the danger, the effects,
The pain, the detriment
It's hurting one's own mind
One's own flesh
One's own heart
One's own love

I repented
I shared ashamed of my conduct
The abuser now the advocate
Against Domestic Violence
It's grievous, it's punishable
It's, undeserved
It kills the spirit, the soul, the flesh
Undermining human regard
Forgetting we are all one and the same! ©

Jaki R Thomas: Educator; Author and Poet

26

Shout

I live with a secret abuser, accuser.
It's mentally draining, physically straining.
He searches my phone when we are alone.
He stops me from seeing my family & friends.
I do not have a social life.
He is a closet bully, always beating me up.
I feel vulnerable, stressed, my life is a toxic mess.
I go through mental torture. I am someone's daughter.
He's nice for a while, but out comes the crocodile,
underneath that lovely smile.
I am a prisoner in my own home. I live in constant fear.
I walk on eggshells, too scared to say or do the wrong thing.
I am black and blue from his energetic thumps and kicks.
He swears at me, threatens me, even says he's gonna kill me.
I want out of this relationship.
I cannot live like this anymore.
I am going to walk right out the door.
I need to protect myself; my children, find a safe home.
I'm scared of what he will do…
I must seek HELP!
I will not stay in it.
I'm gonna run for my life.
Tell someone, anyone, speak out, SHOUT.
Report it to the police get back my peace.
He's too violent.
I will not stay silent. ©

Maureen Morgan: Poetess, Inspirational Speaker, Mentor; Author; Co-author of Women of Faith book and a member of SWWG

27

Silence the Violence

It's everywhere
Violence is a spirit
And not a good one
When will we recognise?
It will not be bound
It will not be stopped
While we bury our heads
And remain in silence

Violence: man to woman
Violence: woman to man
Violence: parent to child
Violence: child to parent
A soul attacked
A seed planted
A seed transferred
A generational curse!

Break yokes, break chains
Sight to the blind
Set the captives free
Violence in the community
Violence in the home
Catch the link?
Rise up and make a noise
Voices against violence
Bind it, rebuke it!

Tear down the stronghold that destroys us all
And cast it out
To bring on healing and take away infirmity

Release the forgiveness
For LIFE is in the tongue, speak up
Silence is deadly (not golden)
Be the change He's called you to be
Faith without works is dead
Raise holy voices to silence the violence, ©

Marcia Barrett: Mindset Coach, Founder of Penworship
Publishers, writer and a member of SWWG

28

The Last Slap

I can still hear the clap as I slapped her face
She went to the cupboard and took out her suitcase
I can still hear the wheels chugging across the floor
She'll be back, she always comes back!

The house is still, a mouse scurries across the floor,
I feel like it's accusing me
No food in the house!
It's been 7 days; she has never been gone this long before
I see her sword upon the floor, she must have dropped it
Hope begins to soar

I open the first page and see my name, along with lots of
bright coloured markings.
The scarlet ribbon catches my eye.

*Colossians 3:19 " Husbands, love your wives and don't treat
them harshly!"*

I read and wept
It's as though I can hear a voice coming from heaven
accusing me
He said, I gave you the apple of my eye
Her name, along with your's are inscribed upon the palm of
my hand
You were supposed to take dominion and multiply

She was never your enemy, but your helpmeet,
Not meet all the plans I still have for you
Which are good and not evil

To give you both hope, a bright future and an expected end

Come to me, and I will heal and restore you both
So, you can love her, as I love all my children
When you are whole and can forgive yourself
I will bring you both back together in Love. ©

Christine Banton: Founder of Azi Sorrel and Chaniel Community Project; Actress; Comedian, Writer and a member of SWWG

29

The start of the end

Will this ever end?
Tired of this toxic cycle
The words exclaimed over me
Are replaying in my head again
As I struggle to forget
All those vicious words that said:
"I am better off dead"
"No one will ever love you"
"You are ugly and worthless"

How did I end up in this mess in the first place?
You said I would always be first place,
I guess, I am the One to blame
Because it was not your fault, it was mine.
I deserved that punch to the face,
The blow to the head, erased the pain of today.
Did I black out again?

Well, that blow to my brain,
Brought me back to my senses.
Enlightened.
Surprised?
We both knew this time I was not meant to arise!

Face all bloodied, bruised
These scars on my face basically spelt out abused.

I am tired of making up excuses
And being used as a personal punching bag!

I refuse to remain in this situation
I choose to end this toxic cycle
I silence the lies of all the negative words
That were exclaimed over me
And recite positive lines of affirmations
Proclaim them till they become my truth
I deserve to live
I am loved
I am beautiful
I answered my first question that was proposed and
I choose to end this and start afresh. ©

Rebekah Stewart (RWAK): Spoken Word Artist, Writer;
Mentor and a member of SWWG

30

There are times

Wait, wait, wait
Let me recompose myself
They've been times when
I engulfed myself emotions inflamed

My, my, my, fists rained blows like thunder
Without lightening
My words in concert with my actions
You see I had it already justified
Anger was enough to left her feeling petrified

Thinking about it now
It must have been confusing for her
Because no two days were the same
Ah mean I expressed lovingness care
Wine and dine, fine foods,
Fine clothes everything was fine
Fine
Fine up to the point of "you anger me"!!!"
Slap, clap, punch!!!!!

Did I feel bad, had regrets, sure I did
But anger was so directed
I had already lost the lid...
Shame now engulfed me...
Trying to reason with self

What, what, what..
What have I done!!!!
What did I do, how,
Why have I done that
To you, to her...

I remembered silence filled the void
I couldn't really explain to myself
The grave I took you, her through

I just couldn't,
Couldn't validate those many times
When there were times that
I violated your dignity your trust...

But I've had times...
There have been times
When I got lost in reflections
Thinking about my then intentions.

There are times
When I, when I, when I wonder
Who have have you become
From the first thunders without lightening

What kind of woman, mother, wife, friend,
daughter you've evolved to be
Whilst I seek forgiveness, time has past...

And so there are times
There are times
There are times
There are times ©

Walk with me

Have you ever wondered
what it's like to be me?
The face of a child, a teen, a woman
At the same time, a body
that has been physically
and mentally broken
with no love for this wasn't enough.

Do they burn like the pain
I feel deep within my heart,
or make you cry when something goes wrong
-The hurting starts,
The noise
the crying
so scared
But I am not lying.

The One who is tortured to the very heart of me
Only I can walk, now look at me.

I want to thank our father of love
for sending a lesson
as if on the wings of a dove
a lesson reminding me that
I should not Deny myself a chance to love
I can walk ©

Juliet Shirley: encourager, please seek God and always talk to
someone

Dear reader, if you have either experienced domestic abuse or would like to support the work against domestic violence, please see the following information below:

AVA (Against Violence & Abuse)
Phone: 020 7549 0273
The Foundry | Office Space and Conference Centre
Address: the Foundry, 17 Oval Way, London SE11 5RR
https://avaproject.org.uk

Back In Control Domestic Abuse Consultancy
Domestic abuse treatment center in London, England
Phone: 020 3150 0171
Address: 65 Sunnyhill Rd, London, SW16 2UG
https://backincontrolconsultancy.com

Black Church Against Domestic Violence
Email: info@bcdaf.org.uk
https://www.bcdaf.org.uk

Mankind
Contact number: 01823 334244
https://www.mankind.org.uk/

Men's Advice Line
Contact number: 0808 801 0327
email info@mensadviceline.org.uk
https://www.womensaid.org.uk

Refuge
Freephone 24-Hour National Domestic Abuse Helpline:
<u>0808 2000 247</u>
or visit <u>www.nationaldahelpline.org.uk</u>

Respect
Contact: 0808 8010327
Email: info@mensadviceline.org.uk
https://mensadviceline.org.uk

Restored
Address: Lytchett House,
13 Freeland Park,
Wareham Road,
Poole,
Dorset, BH16 6FA
Email: info@restored-uk.org
<u>https://www.restored-uk.org</u>

Rise UK
Freedom from abuse & violence
Help number: 01273 622 822
Email: <u>helpline@riseuk.org.uk</u>
Address: RISE
Boundary Road Police Box,
Boundary Road,
Brighton,
BN2 5TJ
<u>https://www.riseuk.org.uk</u>

Samaritans (24/7 service) – 116 123

Sistah Space
Help number: 0207 846 8350
Address: 18 Ashwin Street,
Dalston, E8 3DL
Email: info@sistahspace.org
https://www.sistahspace.org

Women's Aid
Address:
Women's Aid Federation of England,
PO BOX 3245
Bristol,
BS2 2EH, England
Email: helpline@womensaid.org.uk
https://www.womensaid.org.uk

Woman's Trust
Phone: 020 7034 0303
Address: Woman's Trust
PO Box 70420
London NW1W 7GL
Email: office@womanstrust.org.uk
https://womanstrust.org.uk

If in immediate danger Call 999

Further reading:

https://www.faithaction.net

Bonus Poem - I AM here

Submit to your husband
You better bow down
My needs first
You are here to serve
Because of the curse

Bone of my bone
Blamed for the fall of man
The One they wanted to stone
Never mind their own sin
Do as I say, I did exactly that
The head of our home ruled
With an iron fit
He thought he was doing the right thing
Can you argue with the bible

Colossians 3:18 is often quoted
Yet 3:19 is silent

I was torn between my family and friends
The lost was huge, and so was my hair loss
I tried to cover up the historical bruises
And succumbed to the holy hush
Just to cover my spouse
Isn't that what you're supposed to do

I informed our church leaders
And those who were willing to listen
But was always told to forgive him and pray
God will work it out, so I tried, I really did
But the Lord knows, I am not like Jesus

The blows were more than
Forty days and forty nights
I had reached my forgiveness
Of seventy times seventy, times, plus
I was worn out and hung out
What was the message to our children
They were victims too, who thought of them
Who would try and intervene

I prayed hard and daily
But I can truly say,
I am here now, because
I dialed 0808 2000 247 ©

Juliet Daniel: Educator and Psychotherapist, Founder of Poetic
Voices, and SWWG, poet, writer and author ©

To all the writers who have helped to make this anthology possible, thank you:

Heather Annan, Shirley Anthony, Eva Asante, Christine Banton, Marcia Barret, RJ Brown, Kimba Bush-Ramsey, Cherelle, Marlene - Antoinette Daley, Derek Dalson, Janet Edwards, Danzel Hazine, Merlene Huie, Lance G Jones, Jessica Meade, Maureen Morgan, Jade Murray, Nuala Nagle, Naomi, Boy Nash, Andria Rainford, Realitie, Jennifer Ronne, Juliet Shirley, Veronica Simpson, Patrick Stanley (Spoken Man), Rebekah Stewart (RWAK) and Jaki R Thomas.

Printed in Great Britain
by Amazon